50 Transforming Ordinary into Extraordinary Recipes

By: Kelly Johnson

Table of Contents

- Truffle Mac and Cheese
- Caramelized Onion Grilled Cheese
- Balsamic Roasted Strawberries on Yogurt
- Spicy Honey Glazed Fried Chicken
- Garlic Herb Compound Butter Steak
- Maple Bacon Brussels Sprouts
- Loaded Sweet Potato Nachos
- Chili Lime Corn on the Cob
- Brown Butter Chocolate Chip Cookies
- Fig and Goat Cheese Flatbread
- Lemon Zest Pancakes with Berry Compote
- Smoky Paprika Roasted Carrots
- Avocado Egg Salad with Dill
- Caprese Grilled Cheese with Pesto
- Creamy Cajun Shrimp Pasta
- Parmesan Crusted Cauliflower Steaks
- Honey Garlic Roasted Tofu

- Grilled Peach and Burrata Salad
- Crispy Chicken Thighs with Hot Honey
- Butternut Squash Alfredo
- Balsamic Glazed Meatloaf
- Thai Peanut Zoodles
- Cheddar Jalapeño Corn Muffins
- Rosemary Sea Salt Focaccia
- Coconut Lime Rice
- Blackberry Brie Grilled Cheese
- Spiced Apple Pork Chops
- Gnocchi with Brown Butter Sage
- Sriracha Deviled Eggs
- Moroccan Spiced Roasted Chickpeas
- BBQ Pulled Jackfruit Sandwiches
- Sweet and Spicy Roasted Nuts
- Chimichurri Grilled Veggies
- Mango Coconut Chia Pudding
- Korean BBQ Cauliflower Bites
- Baked Feta Pasta with Sun-Dried Tomatoes

- Miso Glazed Eggplant

- Pistachio Crusted Chicken Tenders

- Smoky Chipotle Roasted Potatoes

- Cranberry Orange Glazed Meatballs

- Carrot Ginger Soup with Coconut Cream

- Pear and Blue Cheese Crostini

- Roasted Tomato Garlic Spaghetti

- Bacon-Wrapped Asparagus

- Harissa Roasted Chickpea Bowls

- Baked Apples with Cinnamon Oat Filling

- Lemon Herb Couscous

- Coconut Curry Roasted Cauliflower

- Ricotta Stuffed Shells with Spinach

- Grilled Pineapple with Chili and Lime

Truffle Mac and Cheese

Ingredients:

- 8 oz elbow macaroni
- 2 tbsp butter
- 2 tbsp flour
- 2 cups milk
- 1 cup shredded white cheddar
- 1 cup shredded Gruyère
- 1 tbsp truffle oil (or to taste)
- Salt and pepper to taste
- Optional: breadcrumbs for topping

Instructions:

1. Cook macaroni according to package; drain.
2. In a saucepan, melt butter, whisk in flour to make a roux.
3. Slowly whisk in milk until thickened.
4. Add cheeses, stirring until melted. Mix in truffle oil.
5. Combine with pasta, season to taste. Optional: top with breadcrumbs and broil until golden.

Caramelized Onion Grilled Cheese

Ingredients:

- 4 slices sourdough bread
- 1 cup caramelized onions
- 1 cup shredded Gruyère or sharp cheddar
- 2 tbsp butter

Instructions:

1. Spread butter on one side of each bread slice.
2. Layer cheese and caramelized onions between two slices (buttered sides out).
3. Cook in a skillet over medium heat until golden and cheese is melted, flipping once.

Balsamic Roasted Strawberries on Yogurt

Ingredients:

- 2 cups strawberries (halved)
- 1 tbsp balsamic vinegar
- 1 tbsp honey or maple syrup
- 1/2 tsp vanilla extract
- 1 1/2 cups Greek yogurt

Instructions:

1. Preheat oven to 375°F (190°C). Toss strawberries with balsamic, honey, and vanilla.
2. Roast for 15–20 minutes.
3. Spoon over Greek yogurt. Serve warm or chilled.

Spicy Honey Glazed Fried Chicken

Ingredients:

- 4 chicken thighs or drumsticks
- 1 cup buttermilk
- 1 cup flour
- 1 tsp paprika
- 1/2 tsp cayenne
- Salt and pepper
- Oil for frying

Honey Glaze:

- 1/3 cup honey
- 1 tbsp hot sauce
- 1 tsp apple cider vinegar

Instructions:

1. Marinate chicken in buttermilk for at least 2 hours.
2. Mix flour with spices. Dredge chicken and fry in hot oil until golden and cooked through.
3. Mix glaze ingredients and brush over hot chicken.

Garlic Herb Compound Butter Steak

Ingredients:

- 2 steaks (ribeye, NY strip, etc.)
- Salt and pepper

Compound Butter:

- 1/2 cup butter (softened)
- 2 cloves garlic (minced)
- 1 tbsp parsley
- 1 tsp thyme
- 1/2 tsp lemon zest

Instructions:

1. Mix butter ingredients, roll into a log, chill.
2. Season steaks and sear to desired doneness.
3. Top with a slice of compound butter before serving.

Maple Bacon Brussels Sprouts

Ingredients:

- 1 lb Brussels sprouts (halved)
- 4 slices bacon (chopped)
- 2 tbsp maple syrup
- Salt and pepper

Instructions:

1. Cook bacon until crispy; remove and reserve fat.
2. Sauté Brussels in bacon fat until golden.
3. Add bacon back in, drizzle with maple syrup, and cook another 2–3 minutes.

Loaded Sweet Potato Nachos

Ingredients:

- 2 sweet potatoes (thinly sliced)
- 1 tbsp olive oil
- 1/2 tsp paprika
- 1/2 cup black beans
- 1/2 cup shredded cheese
- 1 avocado (diced)
- Sour cream, jalapeños, green onions for topping

Instructions:

1. Toss sweet potatoes with oil and paprika; roast at 400°F (200°C) for 20–25 minutes.
2. Top with beans and cheese; broil until melted.
3. Add avocado, sour cream, jalapeños, and green onions before serving.

Chili Lime Corn on the Cob

Ingredients:

- 4 ears corn
- 2 tbsp butter
- 1 tsp chili powder
- 1 tbsp lime juice
- Cotija cheese (optional)
- Chopped cilantro

Instructions:

1. Grill or boil corn until tender.
2. Mix butter with chili powder and lime juice.
3. Brush over hot corn. Sprinkle with cheese and cilantro.

Brown Butter Chocolate Chip Cookies

Ingredients:

- 1 cup unsalted butter
- 1 cup brown sugar
- 1/2 cup granulated sugar
- 2 large eggs
- 2 tsp vanilla extract
- 2 1/4 cups all-purpose flour
- 1/2 tsp baking soda
- 1/2 tsp salt
- 1 1/2 cups chocolate chips

Instructions:

1. Brown the butter in a pan until golden and nutty. Let cool slightly.
2. Mix browned butter with sugars until smooth. Add eggs and vanilla.
3. Stir in flour, baking soda, and salt. Fold in chocolate chips.
4. Chill dough for 30 minutes.
5. Scoop onto lined baking sheets and bake at 350°F (175°C) for 10–12 minutes.

Fig and Goat Cheese Flatbread

Ingredients:

- 1 prepared flatbread or naan
- 1/4 cup goat cheese
- 4–5 fresh figs (sliced) or dried (reconstituted)
- 1 tsp honey
- 1/2 tsp rosemary (fresh or dried)
- Arugula (for garnish)
- Olive oil

Instructions:

1. Preheat oven to 400°F (200°C).
2. Brush flatbread with olive oil, top with goat cheese, figs, and rosemary.
3. Bake for 8–10 minutes until golden and crisp.
4. Drizzle with honey and top with fresh arugula before serving.

Lemon Zest Pancakes with Berry Compote

Ingredients (Pancakes):

- 1 1/2 cups flour
- 2 tbsp sugar
- 1 tbsp baking powder
- 1/4 tsp salt
- 1 cup milk
- 2 eggs
- 2 tbsp butter (melted)
- Zest of 1 lemon

Berry Compote:

- 1 cup mixed berries
- 1 tbsp sugar
- 1 tsp lemon juice

Instructions:

1. Mix dry pancake ingredients; in another bowl, mix wet ingredients and zest.
2. Combine and cook pancakes on a greased skillet.
3. For compote: simmer berries, sugar, and lemon juice for 5–7 minutes.
4. Serve pancakes topped with compote.

Smoky Paprika Roasted Carrots

Ingredients:

- 1 lb carrots (peeled and sliced)
- 1 tbsp olive oil
- 1 tsp smoked paprika
- Salt and pepper to taste
- Optional: fresh parsley for garnish

Instructions:

1. Preheat oven to 400°F (200°C).
2. Toss carrots with oil, paprika, salt, and pepper.
3. Roast for 20–25 minutes until tender and caramelized. Garnish if desired.

Avocado Egg Salad with Dill

Ingredients:

- 4 hard-boiled eggs (chopped)
- 1 ripe avocado (mashed)
- 1 tbsp Greek yogurt or mayo
- 1 tsp lemon juice
- 1 tbsp fresh dill (or 1/2 tsp dried)
- Salt and pepper to taste

Instructions:

1. Combine all ingredients in a bowl and mix gently.
2. Serve on toast, in a wrap, or with crackers.

Caprese Grilled Cheese with Pesto

Ingredients:

- 4 slices sourdough bread
- 2 tbsp pesto
- Fresh mozzarella slices
- 1 tomato (sliced)
- Fresh basil leaves
- Butter

Instructions:

1. Butter bread slices on one side. Spread pesto on the other side.
2. Layer mozzarella, tomato, and basil on pesto side. Top with another slice.
3. Grill in a skillet until golden and cheese melts.

Creamy Cajun Shrimp Pasta

Ingredients:

- 8 oz fettuccine or penne
- 1/2 lb shrimp (peeled, deveined)
- 1 tbsp Cajun seasoning
- 1 tbsp butter
- 1/2 cup heavy cream
- 1/4 cup grated Parmesan
- 2 cloves garlic (minced)
- Salt and pepper

Instructions:

1. Cook pasta; drain and reserve 1/2 cup pasta water.
2. Toss shrimp in Cajun seasoning. Sauté in butter until pink. Remove.
3. Add garlic, cream, and Parmesan to pan. Simmer until thickened.
4. Toss in pasta and shrimp. Add pasta water to loosen sauce if needed.

Parmesan Crusted Cauliflower Steaks

Ingredients:

- 1 head cauliflower (cut into 1-inch thick steaks)
- 1/2 cup grated Parmesan
- 1/4 cup breadcrumbs
- 1 tsp garlic powder
- 1 tsp Italian seasoning
- Olive oil

Instructions:

1. Preheat oven to 425°F (220°C). Line a baking sheet.
2. Mix Parmesan, breadcrumbs, and seasonings.
3. Brush cauliflower steaks with oil and press into the crumb mix.
4. Roast for 25–30 minutes until golden and crisp.

Honey Garlic Roasted Tofu

Ingredients:

- 1 block extra-firm tofu (pressed and cubed)
- 2 tbsp soy sauce
- 1 tbsp olive oil
- 1 tbsp cornstarch

Honey Garlic Sauce:

- 2 tbsp honey
- 2 cloves garlic (minced)
- 1 tbsp soy sauce
- 1 tsp rice vinegar
- 1/2 tsp chili flakes (optional)

Instructions:

1. Preheat oven to 400°F (200°C). Toss tofu with soy sauce, olive oil, and cornstarch.
2. Roast for 25–30 min, flipping halfway.
3. In a pan, simmer sauce ingredients until thickened.
4. Toss tofu in sauce and serve hot.

Grilled Peach and Burrata Salad

Ingredients:

- 2 ripe peaches (halved and grilled)
- 1 ball burrata cheese
- Arugula or mixed greens
- 1 tbsp balsamic glaze
- 1 tbsp olive oil
- Salt and pepper

Instructions:

1. Grill peaches until lightly charred.
2. Arrange greens on a plate, top with burrata and peach halves.
3. Drizzle with balsamic glaze and olive oil. Season to taste.

Crispy Chicken Thighs with Hot Honey

Ingredients:

- 4 bone-in, skin-on chicken thighs
- Salt, pepper, paprika
- 1 tbsp olive oil

Hot Honey:

- 1/4 cup honey
- 1 tsp chili flakes
- 1/2 tsp apple cider vinegar

Instructions:

1. Season chicken. Sear skin-side down in oil until crispy.
2. Flip and roast at 425°F (220°C) for 15–20 minutes.
3. Warm hot honey ingredients in a saucepan.
4. Drizzle over chicken before serving.

Butternut Squash Alfredo

Ingredients:

- 2 cups butternut squash (cubed)
- 1/2 cup milk or cream
- 1/4 cup grated Parmesan
- 2 cloves garlic
- 8 oz fettuccine
- Salt, pepper, nutmeg (pinch)

Instructions:

1. Boil squash until soft. Blend with milk, garlic, cheese, salt, and pepper.
2. Cook pasta and toss with sauce. Add a dash of nutmeg for warmth.
3. Serve with extra Parmesan.

Balsamic Glazed Meatloaf

Ingredients:

- 1 lb ground beef or turkey
- 1 egg
- 1/2 cup breadcrumbs
- 1/4 cup milk
- 1/4 cup onion (minced)
- Salt, pepper, thyme

Glaze:

- 2 tbsp balsamic vinegar
- 2 tbsp ketchup
- 1 tbsp brown sugar

Instructions:

1. Mix meatloaf ingredients and shape into a loaf.
2. Bake at 375°F (190°C) for 40 minutes.
3. Brush with glaze, bake 10 more minutes.

Thai Peanut Zoodles

Ingredients:

- 2 zucchinis (spiralized)
- 1/4 cup peanut butter
- 1 tbsp soy sauce
- 1 tbsp lime juice
- 1 tsp sesame oil
- 1/2 tsp grated ginger
- Water to thin

Instructions:

1. Whisk sauce ingredients until smooth.
2. Toss zoodles in sauce, sauté for 2–3 minutes until warm.
3. Garnish with chopped peanuts and cilantro.

Cheddar Jalapeño Corn Muffins

Ingredients:

- 1 cup cornmeal
- 1 cup flour
- 1 tbsp sugar
- 1 tbsp baking powder
- 1/2 tsp salt
- 1 cup milk
- 1 egg
- 1/4 cup butter (melted)
- 1/2 cup shredded cheddar
- 1 jalapeño (chopped)

Instructions:

1. Preheat oven to 375°F (190°C). Mix dry and wet ingredients separately.
2. Combine and fold in cheese and jalapeño.
3. Fill muffin tin and bake 15–18 minutes.

Rosemary Sea Salt Focaccia

Ingredients:

- 2 cups flour
- 1 tsp salt
- 1 tsp sugar
- 1 tsp instant yeast
- 3/4 cup warm water
- 2 tbsp olive oil
- Fresh rosemary and sea salt

Instructions:

1. Mix all dough ingredients, knead 5 minutes.
2. Let rise 1 hour. Spread in oiled pan.
3. Dimple dough, drizzle oil, sprinkle rosemary and salt.
4. Bake at 425°F (220°C) for 20–25 minutes.

Coconut Lime Rice

Ingredients:

- 1 cup jasmine rice
- 1 cup coconut milk
- 3/4 cup water
- Zest and juice of 1 lime
- 1/2 tsp salt
- Optional: chopped cilantro for garnish

Instructions:

1. Rinse rice well. In a pot, combine rice, coconut milk, water, salt, and lime zest.
2. Bring to a boil, reduce heat, cover, and simmer for 15 minutes.
3. Remove from heat, fluff with a fork, stir in lime juice, and garnish if desired.

Blackberry Brie Grilled Cheese

Ingredients:

- 2 slices sourdough or brioche bread
- 2 oz brie cheese
- 2 tbsp blackberry jam or fresh blackberries
- Butter for grilling

Instructions:

1. Butter bread on one side. On the inside, layer brie and blackberry jam or berries.
2. Grill in a pan until golden and cheese is melted. Serve warm.

Spiced Apple Pork Chops

Ingredients:

- 2 boneless pork chops
- 1 apple (thinly sliced)
- 1/2 onion (sliced)
- 1 tbsp olive oil
- 1/2 tsp cinnamon
- Salt, pepper to taste
- Optional: pinch of nutmeg

Instructions:

1. Season pork with salt, pepper, and cinnamon.
2. Sear chops in a pan until golden and cooked through. Remove and set aside.
3. In same pan, sauté onions and apples until tender. Serve over pork chops.

Gnocchi with Brown Butter Sage

Ingredients:

- 1 lb store-bought gnocchi
- 4 tbsp butter
- 6–8 fresh sage leaves
- Salt and pepper
- Grated Parmesan (for topping)

Instructions:

1. Boil gnocchi until they float, then drain.
2. In a skillet, melt butter until golden brown, add sage leaves and crisp.
3. Toss gnocchi in the brown butter. Top with Parmesan.

Sriracha Deviled Eggs

Ingredients:

- 6 hard-boiled eggs
- 3 tbsp mayo
- 1 tsp Sriracha (or to taste)
- 1/2 tsp Dijon mustard
- Salt to taste
- Paprika for garnish

Instructions:

1. Halve eggs and scoop out yolks. Mash yolks with mayo, Sriracha, and mustard.
2. Pipe or spoon filling back into whites. Sprinkle with paprika.

Moroccan Spiced Roasted Chickpeas

Ingredients:

- 1 can chickpeas (drained, rinsed, dried)
- 1 tbsp olive oil
- 1/2 tsp cumin
- 1/2 tsp smoked paprika
- 1/4 tsp cinnamon
- Salt and pepper

Instructions:

1. Preheat oven to 400°F (200°C). Toss chickpeas with oil and spices.
2. Spread on a baking sheet and roast 25–30 minutes until crispy.

BBQ Pulled Jackfruit Sandwiches

Ingredients:

- 1 can young green jackfruit in brine (drained and shredded)
- 1/2 cup BBQ sauce
- 1/4 onion (sliced)
- Olive oil
- Buns for serving

Instructions:

1. Sauté onion in oil, add shredded jackfruit. Cook 5–7 min.
2. Add BBQ sauce and simmer 10–15 minutes.
3. Serve on buns, optionally with slaw.

Sweet and Spicy Roasted Nuts

Ingredients:

- 2 cups mixed nuts
- 1 tbsp honey
- 1 tbsp olive oil
- 1/2 tsp cayenne pepper
- 1/2 tsp smoked paprika
- 1/2 tsp salt

Instructions:

1. Preheat oven to 350°F (175°C). Toss nuts with all ingredients.
2. Spread on baking sheet and roast 12–15 minutes, stirring once.
3. Cool before serving or storing.

Chimichurri Grilled Veggies

Ingredients:

- Assorted vegetables (zucchini, bell peppers, mushrooms, red onion)
- 2 tbsp olive oil
- Salt and pepper

Chimichurri:

- 1/2 cup parsley
- 2 tbsp oregano
- 2 garlic cloves
- 1/4 cup olive oil
- 2 tbsp red wine vinegar
- 1/2 tsp chili flakes
- Salt to taste

Instructions:

1. Blend all chimichurri ingredients until coarse.
2. Toss veggies in oil, salt, and pepper. Grill until tender and slightly charred.
3. Drizzle with chimichurri and serve warm.

Mango Coconut Chia Pudding

Ingredients:

- 1 cup coconut milk
- 1/4 cup chia seeds
- 1 tbsp honey or maple syrup
- 1/2 cup mango (fresh or puréed)

Instructions:

1. Mix coconut milk, chia seeds, and sweetener. Chill for 4 hours or overnight.
2. Stir and layer with mango puree or chunks before serving.

Korean BBQ Cauliflower Bites

Ingredients:

- 1 head cauliflower (florets)
- 1/2 cup flour + 1/2 cup water (batter)
- Korean BBQ sauce (store-bought or homemade)
- Green onions and sesame seeds for garnish

Instructions:

1. Dip cauliflower in batter, bake at 425°F (220°C) for 25 minutes.
2. Toss with Korean BBQ sauce and return to oven for 10 minutes.
3. Garnish and serve.

Baked Feta Pasta with Sun-Dried Tomatoes

Ingredients:

- 1 block feta cheese
- 2 cups cherry tomatoes
- 1/2 cup sun-dried tomatoes
- 3 garlic cloves
- 1/4 cup olive oil
- 8 oz pasta (cooked)
- Fresh basil

Instructions:

1. Place feta, cherry tomatoes, garlic, and sun-dried tomatoes in a baking dish.
2. Drizzle with olive oil, bake at 400°F (200°C) for 30 minutes.
3. Stir in cooked pasta and fresh basil.

Miso Glazed Eggplant

Ingredients:

- 2 small eggplants (halved)
- 2 tbsp white miso paste
- 1 tbsp mirin
- 1 tbsp soy sauce
- 1 tsp sugar
- 1 tsp sesame oil

Instructions:

1. Score eggplant flesh, roast at 400°F (200°C) for 20 minutes.
2. Mix glaze ingredients and brush onto eggplant.
3. Broil 3–5 minutes until caramelized.

Pistachio Crusted Chicken Tenders

Ingredients:

- 1 lb chicken tenders
- 1 cup pistachios (crushed)
- 1/2 cup breadcrumbs
- 2 eggs (beaten)
- Salt, pepper

Instructions:

1. Dip chicken in egg, then in pistachio/breadcrumb mixture.
2. Bake at 400°F (200°C) for 20–25 minutes until golden and cooked through.

Smoky Chipotle Roasted Potatoes

Ingredients:

- 1.5 lbs baby potatoes (halved)
- 2 tbsp olive oil
- 1 tsp chipotle chili powder
- 1/2 tsp smoked paprika
- Salt and pepper

Instructions:

1. Toss potatoes in oil and spices.
2. Roast at 425°F (220°C) for 30–35 minutes until crispy.

Cranberry Orange Glazed Meatballs

Ingredients:

- 1 lb ground turkey or beef
- 1 egg
- 1/4 cup breadcrumbs
- 1/2 tsp garlic powder
- Salt and pepper

Glaze:

- 1/2 cup cranberry sauce
- 1/4 cup orange juice
- 1 tbsp brown sugar

Instructions:

1. Mix meatball ingredients and shape. Bake at 375°F (190°C) for 20 minutes.
2. Simmer glaze ingredients until thickened, toss with cooked meatballs.

Carrot Ginger Soup with Coconut Cream

Ingredients:

- 1 tbsp olive oil
- 1 onion, chopped
- 1 lb carrots, chopped
- 1 tbsp fresh ginger, grated
- 3 cups vegetable broth
- 1 cup coconut milk (plus more for garnish)
- Salt and pepper to taste

Instructions:

1. Sauté onion in oil until soft. Add carrots and ginger, cook 5 minutes.
2. Add broth, bring to a boil, simmer 20 minutes.
3. Blend until smooth. Stir in coconut milk and season. Drizzle extra coconut cream on top to serve.

Pear and Blue Cheese Crostini

Ingredients:

- 1 baguette, sliced
- 2 ripe pears, thinly sliced
- 4 oz blue cheese
- Honey (for drizzling)
- Optional: chopped walnuts

Instructions:

1. Toast baguette slices. Top with pear slices and blue cheese.
2. Drizzle with honey and sprinkle walnuts if using.
3. Broil briefly to slightly melt the cheese.

Roasted Tomato Garlic Spaghetti

Ingredients:

- 8 oz spaghetti
- 2 cups cherry tomatoes
- 4 garlic cloves
- 2 tbsp olive oil
- Fresh basil, salt, and pepper
- Parmesan (for topping)

Instructions:

1. Roast tomatoes and garlic with olive oil at 400°F (200°C) for 25 minutes.
2. Cook pasta, toss with roasted mix and chopped basil.
3. Season and top with Parmesan.

Bacon-Wrapped Asparagus

Ingredients:

- 1 bunch asparagus, trimmed
- 8 slices bacon
- Olive oil, pepper

Instructions:

1. Wrap 3–4 asparagus spears with one bacon slice.
2. Drizzle lightly with oil and pepper.
3. Bake at 400°F (200°C) for 20–25 minutes until crispy.

Harissa Roasted Chickpea Bowls

Ingredients:

- 1 can chickpeas, rinsed and dried
- 1 tbsp olive oil
- 1 tbsp harissa paste
- Cooked quinoa or rice
- Cucumber, cherry tomatoes, greens

Instructions:

1. Toss chickpeas with oil and harissa, roast at 400°F (200°C) for 25 minutes.
2. Serve over grains with fresh veggies.

Baked Apples with Cinnamon Oat Filling

Ingredients:

- 4 apples, cored
- 1/2 cup oats
- 2 tbsp butter
- 2 tbsp brown sugar
- 1/2 tsp cinnamon

Instructions:

1. Mix oats, butter, sugar, and cinnamon. Stuff into apples.
2. Bake at 375°F (190°C) for 30–35 minutes.

Lemon Herb Couscous

Ingredients:

- 1 cup couscous
- 1 cup boiling water
- Zest and juice of 1 lemon
- 1 tbsp olive oil
- 2 tbsp chopped parsley
- Salt and pepper

Instructions:

1. Pour boiling water over couscous, cover and let sit 5 minutes.
2. Fluff and mix with lemon, herbs, oil, and seasoning.

Coconut Curry Roasted Cauliflower

Ingredients:

- 1 head cauliflower, florets
- 2 tbsp coconut milk
- 1 tbsp curry powder
- Salt and pepper

Instructions:

1. Toss cauliflower with coconut milk and curry powder.
2. Roast at 425°F (220°C) for 25–30 minutes.

Ricotta Stuffed Shells with Spinach

Ingredients:

- 12 jumbo pasta shells
- 1 cup ricotta
- 1/2 cup cooked spinach (squeezed dry)
- 1/4 cup Parmesan
- 1 egg
- Marinara sauce

Instructions:

1. Cook shells, mix filling ingredients.
2. Stuff shells and place in baking dish with marinara.
3. Bake at 375°F (190°C) for 25 minutes.

Grilled Pineapple with Chili and Lime

Ingredients:

- 1 pineapple, sliced
- 1 tbsp honey
- 1 tsp chili powder
- Juice of 1 lime

Instructions:

1. Brush pineapple with honey and chili powder.
2. Grill 2–3 minutes per side.
3. Drizzle with lime juice before serving.

www.ingramcontent.com/pod-product-compliance
Lightning Source LLC
LaVergne TN
LVHW081329060526
838201LV00055B/2541